Contents

What is Dinghy Sailing?

Dinghies are small sailing boats. Dinghy sailing has something for everyone – it can be relaxing and fun or fast and exciting. Sailing a dinghy in a light breeze on a lake can be a relaxing way to spend an afternoon. Racing a performance dinghy is a much more exhilarating experience. You have to hang out over the water as you fight to balance the boat and win the race.

All Shapes and Sizes

You can sail a dinghy single-handed or with a crew of one or more other people. Sailors take dinghies out on lakes or on the sea. Dinghies come in a variety of styles and people of all ages, shapes, sizes and abilities can enjoy sailing them. Some boats are made to suit beginners and families. They are designed more for stability than speed. There are lightweight, faster dinghies for those who enjoy speed and excitement.

If you enjoy fast, exhilarating watersports and do not mind the odd dip in the water then dinghy sailing may be the sport for you.

Dinghy
Sailing

Rita Storey

W
FRANKLIN WATTS
LONDON·SYDNEY

First published in 2009 by
Franklin Watts
338 Euston Road
London NW1 3BH

Franklin Watts Australia
Level 17/207 Kent Street
Sydney NSW 2000

© Franklin Watts 2009
Series editor: Jeremy Smith
Art director: Jonathan Hair

Series designed and created for Franklin Watts by Storeybooks.
Designer: Rita Storey
Editor: Nicola Edwards
Photography: John Cleare, Mountain Camera

A CIP catalogue record for this book is available from the British Library.

Dewey classification: 797.1'24
ISBN 978 0 7496 8859 2
Printed in China

Franklin Watts is a division of Hachette Children's Books, an Hachette UK company.
www.hachette.co.uk

Note: At the time of going to press, the statistics in this book were up to date. However, it is possible because of the sailors' ongoing participation in the sport that some of these may now be out of date.

Picture credits
Bigstock pp 7 and 9; Clive Mason/Getty Images p 17 and 24, Don Emmert/AFP/Getty Images p 27; i-stock pp 11, 15, and 26; Shutterstock pp 6, 8 and 9.
Cover image: i-stock

All photos posed by models. Thanks to Owain Hughes, Alice Kingsnorth, Robin Kirby, and Claire Whitehill.

The Publisher would like to thank Tim Cross and the staff at the Mount Batten Sailing Centre, Plymouth for their help. (www.mount-batten-centre.com)

WARNING:
This book is not a substitute for learning from a skilled instructor, which is the only safe way to learn to sail a dinghy.

Sailing can be dangerous if you do not take the correct precautions. If you are spending time on or near water it is vital that you know how to swim.

These young sailors are learning to sail in dinghies that are very stable and difficult to capsize.

Getting Started

If you'd like to try dinghy sailing, the best thing to do is to contact your local sailing club. Many clubs offer 'taster' sessions to those who haven't sailed before so that they can try it for a few hours. For those who want to learn more there are courses available that are run by qualified instructors. The Royal Yachting Association (RYA) in Great Britain runs training courses for all levels of dinghy sailing. The association's 'Sailability' programme gives disabled people access to a variety of sailing activities.

City Sailors

Even if you live in a city, there may be opportunities for you to learn to sail locally. Sailing needn't be an expensive sport to learn. Groups such as 'Sailing for All' and 'Sailing in the City' run programmes that make affordable dinghy sailing possible in some unexpected places. Have a look at the websites on page 29 for more information.

Races and Regattas

As well as a relaxing hobby, dinghy sailing is an exciting competitive sport. Sailing clubs organise races most weekends throughout the summer and a full day of racing, called a regatta, once a year. Races can be for a class or type of dinghy or for a mixed group of boats which race against each other using a handicap system (see page 25) to make it fair. Dinghy sailing at its highest level is an Olympic and Paralymic sport.

Types of Dinghy

Most young dinghy sailors learn to sail in a small cruising dingy or car top dinghy (see page 9). Once they have more experience there are lots of different designs of dinghy to sail.

Dinghy Design

Dinghies can be made of wood, fibreglass or plastic. The shape of the main body of the boat (called the hull), affects how fast you can sail a dinghy. A flat narrow hull will speed across the water but you need to be a competent sailor to keep it upright. A squarer hull that sits lower in the water is less likely to capsize but will not go as fast.

Sails

The larger the size of the sails in proportion to the size of the boat the faster the boat will travel – and the easier it will be to capsize! Some dinghies have only one sail, while others have two sails – a mainsail and a foresail. Sometimes other sails are added for sailing in different conditions. These include spinnakers – the big colourful sails that sailors use when their boats have the wind behind them.

Putting up a spinnaker can make a dinghy move a lot faster.

Cruising Dinghies

Cruising dinghies are designed for leisure sailing. They have smaller sails than other types of dinghy, which makes them slower and less easy to capsize. Cruising dinghies can still be a lot of fun to sail though.

Car Top Dinghies

As their name suggests, car top dinghies can be taken apart and transported on the roof of a car. They are easy to sail and need very little maintenance, and so are used by many sailing schools as a training boat. In the hands of more experienced sailors they can also be exciting dinghies to sail and to race.

Catamarans

Catamarans have two hulls, a high mast and a big sail. These features mean that they can move very fast on the water.

Performance Dinghies

Performance dinghies, called skiffs, are lightweight and have large sails. The 49er is a two-person skiff that became an Olympic sailing class in 2000 (see page 25). Skiffs are the fastest type of dinghy. They are designed to skim along the surface of the water rather than push through it. To balance these boats the crew members lean out over the water using a harness which is attached to the boat by wires. The harness is called a trapeze.

 The crew of this 49er skiff are balancing the power of the wind in the sails by leaning out of the boat on a trapeze.

 A catamaran has two hulls joined together.

Clothing and Equipment

When you first begin to sail you will probably be using a sailing school boat so the only things you need to buy are the right clothes to keep you safe and warm. To start with you will be able to hire most of what you need from the sailing school.

Warm and Flexible

Dinghy sailors who capsize in the winter in ice-cold water are more likely to die of hypothermia than to drown. That makes it vital to have the right sort of protective clothing. Dinghy sailing clothing has been designed to give maximum warmth while using light fabrics that are comfortable and easy to move around in.

This outfit would keep this sailor warm even if her boat capsized in very cold water.

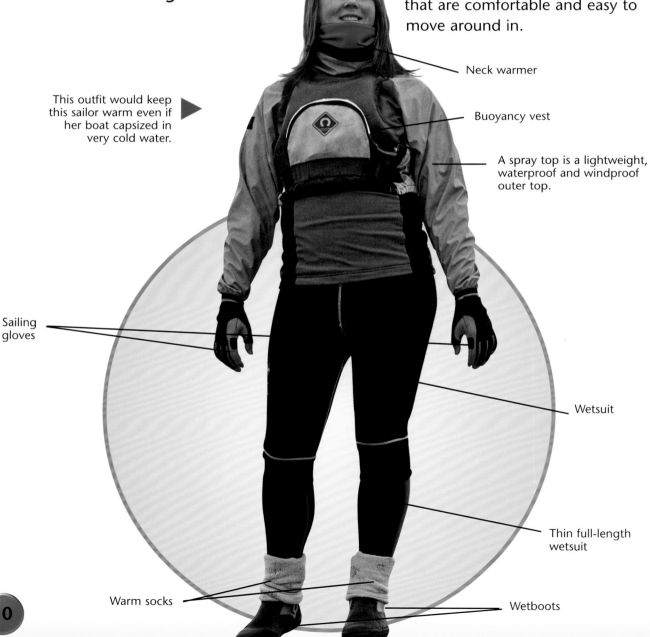

Neck warmer

Buoyancy vest

A spray top is a lightweight, waterproof and windproof outer top.

Sailing gloves

Wetsuit

Thin full-length wetsuit

Warm socks

Wetboots

Dinghy sailors need to be able to move around the boat very quickly. They wear clothes that allow them to do this while keeping them warm.

You will need to wear:

- A waterproof outer layer. This can be a wetsuit, a drysuit or a waterproof top and trousers. Wetsuits let in a small amount of water that warms up next to your body. Drysuits have seals at the neck, wrists and ankles that keep all the water out.
- A warm middle layer to keep in your body heat.
- An under layer. Sailing is an energetic sport and in a hour of moderate exercise our bodies give off half a litre of sweat. Modern materials worn next to your skin draw the sweat away from your skin and stop you feeling damp and uncomfortable.
- A good pair of sailing gloves keep your hands warm and stop them getting sore when you pull on the ropes.
- Dinghy sailing boots to keep your feet dry. The soles of these boots are designed to grip the deck to stop you slipping.

Safety Equipment

- A buoyancy vest is a vital piece of safety equipment for all dinghy sailors however well they can swim. It must fit well and not come off if you fall in the water. A buoyancy vest will not keep you afloat in the same way as a lifejacket, but it will help.
- When you are learning to sail, the sailing school will provide a helmet to protect you if you hit your head on the boom (see page 12) as it swings across.

Top Tip

To avoid damaging your wet suit when you are sailing, wear a protective layer over the top. Shorts, a spray suit or hiking trousers will all offer protection.

Rigging a Dinghy

Before you can sail a dinghy it has to be rigged. Rigging means putting together the parts of the boat that have been taken off while the dinghy has been stored.

Before you start

First of all you need to make sure that your boat is watertight. All open boats will collect water. Dinghies have holes in the hull to let the water out when you are sailing. The holes are closed with a flap or a plug (called a bung). If these holes are left open they can let in water. You will need to close the flaps and put in the bungs before you start to rig your boat.

The Boom, Mast and Sails

A car top boat like the one below ('a Topper') may have its mast and boom taken off so that the boat can be stowed flat on a roof rack. This means that you have to put them back on each time you use the boat. Other types of dinghy may be stored with the mast in place.

Some dinghies have only one sail that is stored rolled round the mast. On other types of boat the sail is pulled up the mast using a rope called a halyard.

Parts of a Dinghy

Mast The vertical pole to which the mainsail is attached.

Boom The horizontal pole to which the bottom of the mainsail is attached.

Tiller This moves the rudder to steer the boat.

Cockpit The part of the boat in which the members of the crew sit.

Kicker The connecting piece of rope or wire between the boom and the mast. It stops the boom from rising up.

Bow The front of the boat

Rudder This goes into the water at the back of the boat and is used to steer the boat.

Launching trolley A frame with wheels and a handle that the boat sits on so that it can be moved around on land.

Stern The back of the boat

Hull The main body of the boat

Daggerboard This is a board that is dropped down into a slot in the bottom of the boat when the boat is sailing. It helps to keep the boat upright.

Rigging a Car Top Dinghy

1 *Slot the mast into the hole in the hull and lock it in place. Unroll the sail.*

2 *Clip the boom onto the mast.*

Boom

Kicker

Mast

3 *Attach the sail to the end of the boom.*

4 *Fix the kicker between the boom and the mast.*

5 *Attach the rope that controls the mainsail (also known as the mainsheet) to the end of the boom.*

6 *Slot the rudder and tiller into position. Keep the rudder upright until the boat is in the water.*

13

Launching a Dinghy

Once you've rigged your boat it's ready to be launched. In a sailing club you'll probably use a gradual slope built into the water, called a slipway, to launch your boat. The easiest way to get a small dinghy into the water is to push it down the slipway on a launching trolley (see page 12).

Launching from a Slipway

1 Push the trolley down the slipway into the water. There needs to be enough water under the boat to float the dinghy. Point the dinghy so that the wind is blowing from from bow to stern (this is called 'head-to-wind'). Hold onto the dinghy while someone takes the trolley away.

2 Push the daggerboard into the slot in the bottom of the boat. Make sure that the daggerboard is attached to the mast to stop it falling off if the boat capsizes.

3 Put the rudder down. Move the boat so that the wind is blowing across it. The sail will flap. Climb in. You are now ready to sail away.

Be Prepared

In the summer, when lots of people want to launch their boats, slipways can get very crowded. Before you take your dinghy down the slipway check that it is properly rigged and ready to sail. Make sure that you have everything you need so that you can launch quickly and smoothly without holding other people up.

You may need someone to help you by:
- Holding the trolley while you float the dinghy off it.
- Holding the dinghy while you get into it.
- Taking the trolley back to the trolley park to leave the slipway clear for other users.

Take Care

Never jump into a dinghy when it is still on land. Without the support of the water under it your weight may make a hole in the bottom of the boat.

There may not always be a handy slipway from which to launch your dinghy. These sailors are carrying their dinghy to launch it from the beach.

Balancing the Boat

To get the best performance out of a dinghy the helmsman and crew need to work together as a team. They must control the sails, hull, daggerboard and rudder correctly to keep the boat in balance.

Who does what?

The helmsman is in charge of the boat. He or she controls the mainsail and the tiller and gives instructions to the crew. The crew sits further forward and controls the daggerboard, the jib (foresail) sheet and any additional sails that are used.

Balance

A boat that is sailing at a very steep angle will sail more slowly than one sailing at a slight angle. Keeping the boat in balance from side to side can be a difficult job especially in a fast moving performance dinghy. Both crew members must be constantly aware of where their weight needs to be and change position if necessary. They hook their feet under straps that are fixed to the boat to stop them falling out as they lean right out over the water.

Boat Trim

The trim is the balance of the boat from front to back. To keep the trim level the crew members move nearer to the front or back of boat depending on the point of sail (see page 23).

The steep angle of this boat means that the crew will not be able to move at great speed.

Sails

It's important to use the right amount of sail for the size of your boat and the conditions in which you are sailing. If you use too much sail in breezy conditions, a sudden gust will tip your boat over. Using too little sail will mean that the boat will not go as fast as it could. On some boats you can roll the sail around the mast to make it smaller. Other boats have reefing lines attached to the sail. When you pull on these lines it creates a fold in the sail, making it smaller.

Single-handed

If you are sailing a dinghy single-handed you will have to control the balance and trim of the boat and its sails all by yourself.

Pippa Wilson, Sarah Webb and Sarah Ayton of Great Britain compete on their way to victory in the Yngling class event at the 2008 Olympic Games in Beijing.

Pippa Wilson MBE

Date of birth: February 7th, 1986

Nationality: British

Sailing Class: Yngling

2008 – Olympic gold medal

2007 – ISAF World Championships – gold medal

Sarah Webb MBE

Date of birth: January 13th, 1977

Nationality: British

Sailing Class: Yngling

2008 – Olympic gold medal

2007 – ISAF World Championship – gold medal

2004 – Olympic gold medal

Sarah Ayton MBE

Date of birth: April 9th,1980

Nationality: British

Class - Yngling

2008 – Beijing Olympics – Gold medal

2007 – ISAF World Championships – Gold medal

2004 - Athens Olympic Games – Gold medal

Sarah Ayton, Sarah Webb and Pippa Wilson can compete in any weather conditions. They won their gold medals in Beijing in high winds and choppy seas.

Safety

Dinghies are kept upright using the body weight of the crew balanced against the force of the wind in the sails. If your boat isn't balanced you may capsize. It's vital to know what to do if you capsize and how to get your boat upright again safely.

Righting a Dinghy

If you capsize the worst that is likely to happen is that you will get wet. Your buoyancy vest will help keep you afloat. Dinghies are designed to be righted quickly and easily. Keep calm so that you will be able to think clearly and remember what to do. Practise capsizing and righting your boat when the weather is good. That way you will know what to do and be able to react quickly if you capsize in bad weather or during a race.

Righting a Capsized Dinghy

This way of righting a dinghy is called the scoop method. The crew member is scooped up inside the boat as the helmsman pulls it upright. If you are sailing single handed you need to do what the helmsman is doing below.

▼

1 *The helmsman (on the left) knows that the dinghy is going to capsize and is taking action. He is climbing out as the boat tips over.*

2 *The helmsman stands on the daggerboard as close to the hull of the boat as possible and uses his weight to pull the boat upright. The crew member holds on to the inside of the boat.*

Man Overboard Drill

If you sail a two-person dinghy it is important to practise what to do if one of you falls overboard. Both crew members need to be able to handle the boat so that they can sail back to the person in the water and get him or her back into the boat as quickly as possible.

Stay Safe

All dinghies are designed with added buoyancy so they should not sink. If you find you can't right your boat you should stay with it rather than try to swim to the shore. A capsized dinghy is easier to spot than a lone swimmer and you may be further from the shore than you think.

▲ If you are sailing at a sailing club there will always be someone on the water in a safety boat to help you if you get into difficulties.

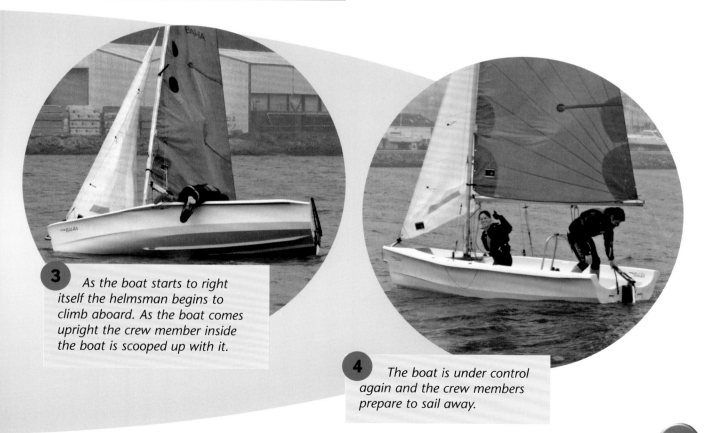

3 *As the boat starts to right itself the helmsman begins to climb aboard. As the boat comes upright the crew member inside the boat is scooped up with it.*

4 *The boat is under control again and the crew members prepare to sail away.*

Tacking

A dinghy is moved by the wind. As a sailor you must learn to use the strength and direction of the wind to get the best performance from your boat. If you don't understand what the wind is doing you may struggle to make any progress or put yourself at risk of capsizing.

Straight Ahead

You cannot sail any boat straight into the wind. If you try to aim your boat towards the wind it will stop and may even start to go backwards.

If you want to go straight ahead and the wind is blowing towards you (upwind), you will need to sail a zig-zag course. Turning a boat across the wind is called tacking. When you turn the boat, the wind will move the boom from one side of the boat to the other and the mainsail will fill with wind on the other side of the boat. As the boat turns the crew members have to move across to the other side of the boat to balance it. They also need to adjust the sails on the new course.

Tacking

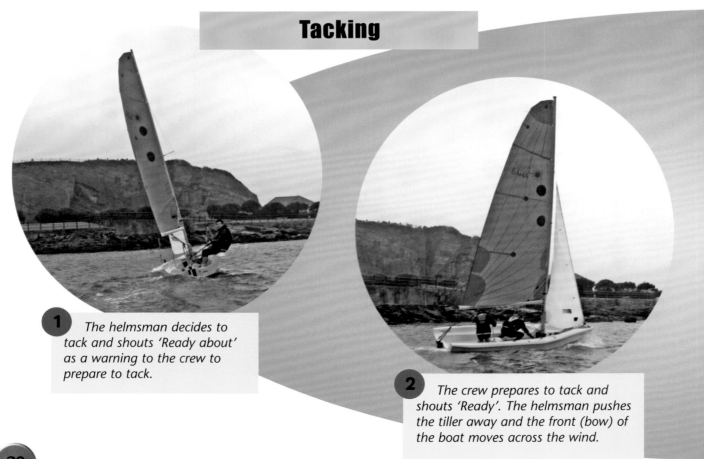

1 The helmsman decides to tack and shouts 'Ready about' as a warning to the crew to prepare to tack.

2 The crew prepares to tack and shouts 'Ready'. The helmsman pushes the tiller away and the front (bow) of the boat moves across the wind.

The person at the helm who steers the boat is responsible for letting the other crew members know when he or she is about to change to another tack. First the helmsman will shout 'Ready about' as a warning to the crew to prepare to tack. When they are prepared they will reply 'Ready' and the helmsman will push the tiller away from him and shout 'Lee-oh' to let the crew know that they are changing direction. They will loosen the ropes attached to the sails to allow the sails to move across to the other side of the boat.

As the boat turns into the wind, all the crew members (including the helmsman) move to the opposite side of the boat to balance it.

Port and Starboard

When you are inside a boat facing the front the starboard side is on the right and the port side is on the left. When you are tacking the wind will be blowing over one side of the boat. When it is blowing over the starboard side you are on a starboard tack and if it is blowing over the port side you are on a port tack.

Watch Out!

Listen to the instructions from the helmsman. When you change course, the boom will swing across the boat. Be ready to duck if necessary to avoid a sore head!

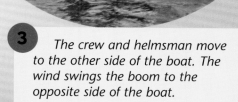

3 *The crew and helmsman move to the other side of the boat. The wind swings the boom to the opposite side of the boat.*

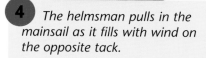

4 *The helmsman pulls in the mainsail as it fills with wind on the opposite tack.*

Gybing

Gybing is the term used for changing course when you have the wind behind you (downwind). It can be a noisy and dangerous manoeuvre as the boom can swing violently from one side of the boat to the other.

Gybing Safely

If you are sailing with the wind behind you the boom and the sail will be out over one side of the boat. As you gybe, the stern of the boat will go across the wind and the boom and sails will move across to the other side of the boat. Gybing happens very fast and can make the boat unbalanced even in light winds.

Accidental Gybing

If the helmsman does not steer a steady course when sailing downwind the boat can gybe accidentally. This can be dangerous as, without any warning, the crew may get hit by the boom as it swings across.

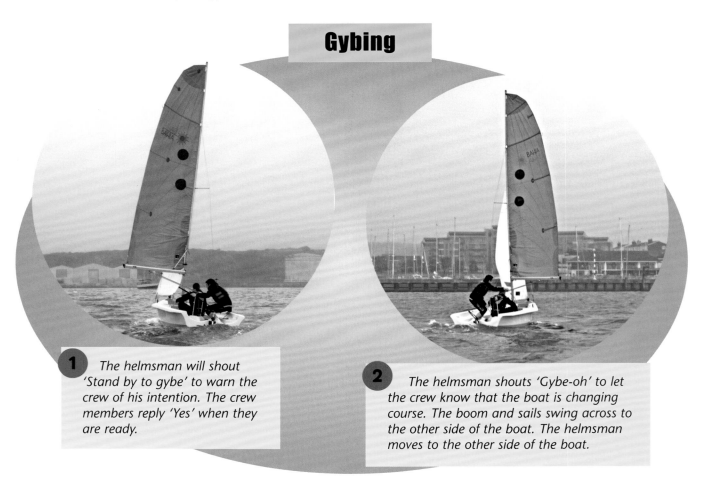

Gybing

1 *The helmsman will shout 'Stand by to gybe' to warn the crew of his intention. The crew members reply 'Yes' when they are ready.*

2 *The helmsman shouts 'Gybe-oh' to let the crew know that the boat is changing course. The boom and sails swing across to the other side of the boat. The helmsman moves to the other side of the boat.*

Direction

When you are sailing you need to angle the sails in different ways depending on the wind and the direction in which you want to travel.

Close-hauled

The nearest you can get to sailing directly into the wind in a sailing boat is with the boat and sails at an angle of 45° to the wind blowing towards it (upwind).

Beam Reach

On a beam reach the boat is at right angles to the direction of the wind.

Broad Reach

On a broad reach the boat is at 45° to the wind with the wind behind it (downwind)

Run

This when the wind is directly behind the boat (downwind). The sails should be full out.

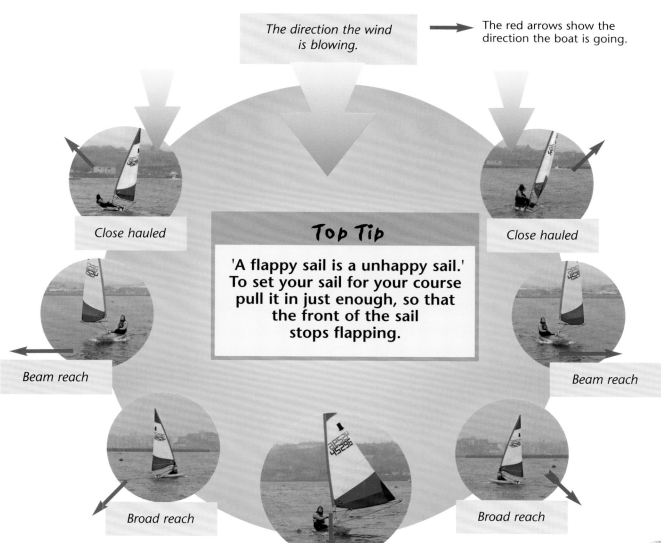

The direction the wind is blowing.

The red arrows show the direction the boat is going.

Close hauled

Close hauled

Top Tip

'A flappy sail is a unhappy sail.'
To set your sail for your course pull it in just enough, so that the front of the sail stops flapping.

Beam reach

Beam reach

Broad reach

Broad reach

Run

Dinghy Racing

▲ Representing the USA, Anna Tunnicliffe won the gold medal in the Women's Laser Radial sailing class at the 2008 Olympics.

Dinghy sailing is a competitive sport at every level, from handicap races at a local sailing club to the top international and Olympic events.

Anna Tunnicliffe

Date of birth: October 17th 1982

Nationality: American

Sailing Class: Single-handed Laser Radial

2008 – Olympic gold medal

2009 – ISAF Sailing World Cup Series
Sail Melbourne
Rolex Miami

Anna Tunnicliffe was a top sailor throughout senior school. She is also a talented athlete. In her final year at school she won district track championships in the 800 metres and set a new high school record of 2 minutes 17.56 seconds.

One Design
When dinghies that are exactly the same race each other they are called 'one design' classes. The aim of this type of racing is that no boat should have any advantage over another. As a result, the winner should be the crew with the greatest sailing ability rather than the crew with the best boat. People race boats of all types in this way at all levels, nationally and internationally.

Handicap Races
In a handicap event competitors of different ages and abilities and boats of different classes can compete against each other with an equal chance of winning. A system of time penalty handicaps adjusts the time each boat takes to finish a course so that the boat that finishes first does not always win the race.

International Dinghy Racing
Dinghy racing worldwide is organised by the International Sailing Federation (ISAF). Sailors compete in national and international races around the world in the run up to competitions such as the ISAF Sailing World Championships and the Youth World Championships.

Watch Out!
All the dinghies in a race are propelled by the wind. Beware: if another dinghy gets between the wind and your boat the wind will fill its sails and not yours – and this will slow you right down.

Olympic Competition
Sailing competition at the Olympic Games is organised by classes, or types of boat. In any race, only boats of the same class may compete against each other. The Olympic classes are for single-handed, double-handed or three-person boats and can be either women's, men's or open (see below) disciplines.

Open Class
Open classes are for both men and women. In an open class the boats can be modified. There can be differently designed sails and masts. A boat that has been skillfully modified can give its crew the edge over another crew who may have greater sailing ability.

Olympic Dinghy Sailing Events
- 470 – Two-Person Dinghy (Men)
- Laser – One-Person Dinghy (Men)
- Star – Keelboat (Men)
- 470 – Two-Person Dinghy (Women)
- Laser Radial – One-Person Dinghy (Women)
- Yngling – Keelboat (Women)
- 49er – Skiff (Mixed)
- Finn – Heavyweight Dinghy (Mixed)
- Tornado – Multihull (Mixed)

Racing Rules and Tactics

Once they have some basic experience, most dinghy sailors will want to try racing their boat against others. Racing adds an element of excitement to sailing. It is a good idea to learn some basic racing rules before you start to avoid upsetting your competitors.

Racing Rules

A dinghy race is sailed round brightly-coloured marks or buoys that are positioned to make a course. There are 90 different rules that govern dinghy racing but the most important to learn are about who has right of way. Officials at any sailing club that runs races will talk you through what you need to know before you start to race. Knowing the right-of-way rules is particularly important when several boats are going round one of the marks. If you obstruct another boat you may be disqualified. You also need to know the system of sound signals and flags that the race organisers use to communicate with the competitors out on the water.

A Good Start

Your race tactics need to focus on being at the start line in the right place and at the right time. If your boat is miles away from the start line when the race starts it will make it difficult for you to win the race. Boats that are already sailing at top speed when the start signal goes, will have an advantage over the boats that still have to accelerate up to speed.

However, you need careful timing – if you misjudge it and are over the line at the start signal, you will have to go back and cross the line again. Any boat that does not start correctly is disqualified.

In very light winds there is a danger of being becalmed away from the start line and unable to move. In these conditions you should stay as close as you can to the start line.

When lots of dinghies are all aiming for the same marks in windy conditions boats can collide. You need to know what to do to avoid a collision.

Ben Ainslie of Great Britain sails round a mark on his way to winning a gold medal in the Sailing Finn class at the 2008 Olympics.

Trim

To ensure that their dinghy is sailing at its fastest the crew members need to be in the right place in the boat. Usually it is best to sit well forward when sailing towards the wind and further back when sailing away from the wind.

Hitting the Mark

Choosing the right course to each racing mark takes practise and experience. To get it right you have to understand the wind and the changing conditions. Try to see what course other sailors are on so that you can learn from their experience.

Ben Ainslie OBE

Date of birth: February 5th 1977

Nationality: British

Sailing Class: Finn

2008 – Olympic gold medal, Single-handed Dinghy (Finn)

2004 – Olympic gold medal Single-handed Dinghy (Finn)

2000 – Olympic gold medal Single-handed Dinghy (Laser)

1996 – Olympic silver medals Single-handed Dinghy (Laser)

Ben Ainslie is an exceptionally talented dinghy sailor. He competed in his first Olympics in 1996 when he was 19 years old, taking home the silver medal in the Laser class. He won the world championships in 1998 and 1999 in the same class and then a gold medal in the Sydney Olympics in 2000. He switched to the Finn class in 2002 and won three consecutive world championships. He went on to win an Olympic gold medal in Athens in 2004 (even though a disqualification had left him right at the back of the pack and he had to make a remarkable comeback). He won another gold medal in Beijing in 2008.

He was awarded the MBE (Member of the Order of the British Empire) in 2001, the OBE (Officer of the Order of the British Empire) in 2005 and the CBE (Commander of the Order of the British Empire) in 2009.

Record Holders

Event	Gold	Silver	Bronze
Laser class	Paul Goodison Great Britain	Vasilij Zbogar Slovenia	Diego Romero Italy
470 class	Nathan Wilmot Malcolm Page Australia	Nick Rogers Joe Glanfield Great Britain	Nicolas Charbonnier Olivier Bausset France
Star class	Iain Percy Andrew Simpson Great Britain	Robert Scheidt Bruno Prada Brazil	Fredrik Lööf Anders Ekström Sweden

Women's Olympic Champions, 2008 Beijing

Event	Gold	Silver	Bronze
Laser Radial class	Anna Tunnicliffe United States	Gintarò Volungeviciute Lithuania	Xu Lijia China
470 class	Elise Rechichi Tessa Parkinson Australia	Marcelien de Koning Lobke Berkhout Netherlands	Fernanda Oliveira Isabel Swan Brazil
Yngling class	Sarah Ayton Sarah Webb Pippa Wilson Great Britain	Mandy Mulder Annemieke Bes Merel Witteveen Netherlands	Sofia Bekatorou Sofia Papadopoulou Virginia Kravarioti Greece

Open Event Olympic Champions, 2008 Beijing

Event	Gold	Silver	Bronze
Finn class	Ben Ainslie Great Britain	Zach Railey United States	Guillaume Florent France
49er class	Jonas Warrer Martin Kirketerp Denmark	Iker Martínez de Lizarduy Xabier Fernández Spain	Jan-Peter Peckolt Hannes Peckolt Germany
Tornado class	Antón Paz Fernando Echavarri Spain	Darren Bundock Glenn Ashby Australia	Santiago Lange Carlos Espínola Argentina

Glossary

Balance To be equal on both sides.

Becalmed Unable to move the boat because there is no wind.

Bow The front of a boat.

Bungs Plugs used to close a hole.

Capsize To turn the boat upside down or on its side.

Crew All the people sailing a boat. Some members of the crew, such as the helmsman, have specific jobs.

Daggerboard A piece of wood, fiberglass, or metal that is dropped down into a slot in the bottom of the boat when the boat is sailing. It helps to keep the boat upright.

Foresail The sail nearest to the front of the boat.

Gybe To change direction by turning the back of the boat through the wind.

Hypothermia Dangerously low body temperature caused by exposure to cold conditions.

Jib A triangular headsail in front of the mast.

Kicker The connecting piece of rope or wire between the boom and the mast. It stops the boom from rising up.

Mast The vertical pole to which the mainsail is attached.

Mainsail The sail attached to the boom.

Mainsheet The rope that controls the boom.

Port The left side of a boat, looking forward towards the bow.

Righting Getting a boat upright

Rudder The vertical metal or wooden plate attached to the stern, the movements of which steer the boat.

Slipway a gradual slope built into the water used to launch a boat.

Starboard The right side of a boat, looking forward towards the bow.

Stern The back of a boat.

Tack To change direction by turning the front of the boat through the wind.

Tiller A piece of wood connected to the rudder. It is used to steer the boat.

Trim The balance of a boat from front to back.

Websites

http://www.scils.rutgers.edu/~elfox/terms.html
This website has a list of basic terms used in sailing.

www.sailingforall.com
A list of access dinghies courses. These are designed to appeal to all those who want to have a go at sailing.

www.sailing.org/isafsailing worldcup
The official website of the International Sailing Federation has up-to-date information about all the ISF events. Click on the 'Connect to sailing' button to find details of how to get started in sailing.

www.rya.org.uk
The official RYA site has the latest information on where to find sailing courses for beginners.

http://www.go-sail.co.uk/homedinghy.asp
From classes of dinghies to training courses this site has a lot of useful information.

www.yachting.org.au
This site has information about the national small boat training scheme for sailors in Australia.

www.wpnsa.org.uk/
Keep up to date with what is happening at the UK's sailing venue for the 2012 Olympics.

Note to parents and teachers: every effort has been made by the Publishers to ensure that these websites are suitable for children, that they are of the highest educational value, and that they contain no inappropriate or offensive material. However, because of the nature of the Internet, it is impossible to guarantee that the contents of these sites will not be altered. We strongly advise that Internet access is supervised by a responsible adult.

Index